EDGE BOOKS™

TRUE TALES OF SURVIVAL PRESENTS:

LEFT FOR DEAD!

LINCOLN HALL'S STORY OF SURVIVAL

WITHDRAWN

by Tim O'Shei

Consultant:
Al Siebert, PhD
Author of *The Survivor Personality*

Capstone press®

Mankato, Minnesota

Edge Books are published by Capstone Press,
151 Good Counsel Drive, P.O. Box 669, Mankato, Minnesota 56002.
www.capstonepress.com

Library of Congress Cataloging-in-Publication Data
O'Shei, Tim.
    Left for dead!: Lincoln Hall's story of survival / by Tim O'Shei.
    p. cm.—(Edge. True tales of survival)
    Includes bibliographical references and index.
    ISBN-13: 978-1-4296-0090-3 (hardcover)
    ISBN-10: 1-4296-0090-X (hardcover)
    1. Hall, Lincoln, 1955– 2. Mountaineers—Australia—Biography—Juvenile
literature 3. Mountaineering—Everest, Mount (China and Nepal)—Juvenile
literature. 4. Survival—Juvenile literature. I. Title. II. Series.
GV199.92.H3235O84 2008
796.522092—dc22   2007004901

Summary: Describes the rescue of Lincoln Hall after he was stranded overnight
near the top of Mount Everest.

Editorial Credits
Mandy Robbins, editor; Jason Knudson, set designer; Kyle Grenz, book designer;
    Charlene Deyle and Deirdre Barton, photo researchers

Photo Credits
AP/Wide World Photos, 28
© Harry Kikstra, 7summits.com, 4–5, 8–9, 10, 13, 14–15, 16, 18, 20–21, 24,
    26, 27, 29
The Image Works/Topham, 6
Jamie McGuinness - Project-Himalaya.com, 23
Shutterstock/ANP, back cover; Bruce Yeung, cover, 24–25 (background), 32;
    Jason Maehl, 6–7 (background), 10–11 (background), 12–13 (background),
    18–19 (background), 22–23 (background), 26–27 (background),
    28–29 (background); Pichugin Dmitry, 1, 16–17 (background); wu xiao bai, 30

1 2 3 4 5 6 12 11 10 09 08 07

TABLE OF CONTENTS

CHAPTER 1

A RUDE AWAKENING

LEARN ABOUT:

- Stranded on Everest
- Adventure gone bad
- Lincoln's promise to his family

4

Lincoln Hall's eyes popped open. Everything around him was black. The ice-cold air bit into his skin. Lincoln saw that he was sitting in snow. His fingers and toes were so frostbitten, they felt more like wood than flesh.

Slowly, Lincoln remembered where he was. Weeks earlier, he had left his home in Australia for Mount Everest. Everest is the tallest mountain in the world. Lincoln was part of a team of climbers aiming to reach Everest's highest point or summit. Just one day earlier, Lincoln had done it. But his trip back down the mountain had taken some bad turns.

Now, Lincoln was stranded. He was sitting on a cliff—with nowhere to go.

6

Sir Edmund Hillary reached Everest's summit at 11:30 on the morning of May 29, 1953.

British climber Sir Edmund Hillary and his Sherpa, Tenzing Norgay, were the first people to reach the summit of Mount Everest.

The air was thin. Without enough oxygen, Lincoln couldn't think clearly. But he did remember a promise he had made to his family. Lincoln had sworn to his wife and sons that he would return safely. Lincoln was afraid he wouldn't be able to keep that promise.

7

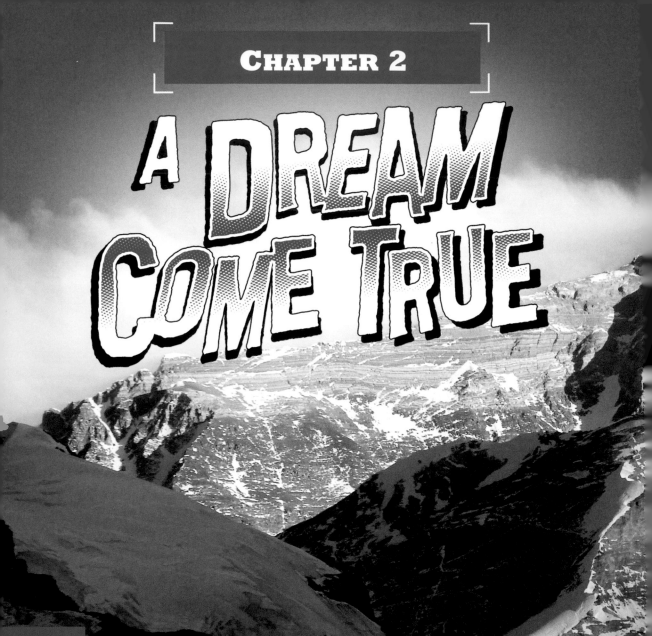

CHAPTER 2

A DREAM COME TRUE

8

LEARN ABOUT:

- Second shot at the summit
- Joining the team
- Climbers become ill

Australian Lincoln Hall began climbing at age 15. He had explored the mountains of New Zealand, the Andes, and the Himalayas. In 1984, he almost reached the top of Mount Everest. His dream was to try again.

Twenty-two years after his first attempt, Lincoln got a second chance. A 15-year-old named Christopher Harris wanted to become the youngest person to climb Mount Everest. Christopher's father, Richard, asked Lincoln to guide them on the trip.

Mount Everest is one of the most dangerous places on Earth. Its cold temperatures have killed many skilled climbers. Even more deadly is the altitude. Everest stands nearly 6 miles (9.7 kilometers) high. The air is so thin at the top of Everest that walking a few steps can be exhausting. The lack of oxygen can make a person's brain swell and lungs shut down.

Climbing to the top of Mount Everest takes supreme skill, fitness, and courage. Though he was 50 years old, Lincoln was confident he could do it. He had been a climber for most of his life and was in top physical condition. Lincoln left for his trip in April 2006. But first he promised his wife, Barbara, and sons, Dorje and Dylan, that he would make it home alive.

Lincoln was determined to make it to the top of Mount Everest this time.

STARTING THE EXPEDITION

Lincoln's trip began in Kathmandu, Nepal. There, he met with Richard and Christopher Harris. Later, they joined other members of the team, including leader Alex Abramov. The team also included Thomas Weber, a visually impaired climber. He was climbing Everest to raise money for charity. A camera crew joined Weber to film a documentary about the expedition.

The team drove from Nepal to a Mount Everest base camp in Tibet. They camped in tents there for five weeks. The climbers needed to give their bodies a chance to adjust to the 17,000-foot (5,200-meter) altitude.

He had been a climber for most of his life and was in top physical condition.

TO THE TOP

In mid-May, the team left base camp accompanied by Sherpas. These local experts help Mount Everest climbers in dangerous situations.

Lincoln felt strong and fit, but not everyone was doing so well. By the time the team reached 22,000 feet (6,700 meters), Richard Harris was coughing constantly and couldn't keep food down. Richard's trip was over. He climbed down 4,000 feet (1,200 meters) to a camp where the air had more oxygen.

Richard's son Christopher tried to continue. He reached 23,000 feet (7,000 meters) before getting sick. A doctor ordered Christopher to return to base camp. The teenager's trip was over too.

EDGE FACT

Sherpas are a group of people who live in the Himalayan region. They are often employed by climbers to help on dangerous trips.

Still feeling strong, Lincoln kept climbing. Each week he used a satellite phone to check in with Barbara. On May 25, he called her with exciting news. He was only hours from the summit of Mount Everest. Lincoln's lifelong dream was about to come true.

Sherpas are an important part of most climbing teams on Mount Everest.

CHAPTER 3

LOSING GROUND

LEARN ABOUT:

- The Death Zone
- From a dream to a nightmare
- Left for dead

14

Lincoln felt strong as he neared
the summit of Mount Everest.

On Mount Everest, the area above 26,000 feet (7,900 meters) is called the Death Zone. Climbers in the Death Zone sometimes don't think clearly. The air there contains one-third the oxygen it would have at sea level. The lack of oxygen makes it difficult for climbers to stay physically and mentally sharp.

Most climbers have spent years planning for their Everest climb. Many of them have paid a small fortune for the trip. When climbers reach the Death Zone, they are incredibly close to the summit. After spending so much time and money, they are determined to reach the top. Climbers have ignored others who need help just to achieve their goal. Earlier in May 2006, a climber named David Sharp froze to death while 40 climbers passed by him.

As an experienced climber, Lincoln knew that staying clearheaded on Everest is a challenge. That's why reaching the summit is so rewarding. It's also why staying on top too long can be deadly.

The medical name for altitude sickness is cerebral oedema.

16

Altitude sickness even strikes Sherpas, who have lived all their lives at high altitudes. This memorial honors Sherpas who have died on Mount Everest.

When Lincoln reached the top of Mount Everest on May 25, he was thrilled. He had reached his lifelong goal. But his trip was only half over. He still had to climb down the mountain. Lincoln had already spent hours in the Death Zone. The longer he was there, the more danger he was in.

As Lincoln began his descent, a Sherpa delivered bad news. Thomas Weber, the visually impaired climber, had fallen behind. He had collapsed in the snow saying, "I'm dying." Shortly after that, he died. Thomas was the second member of the expedition to die. A climber named Igor Plyushkin had died days earlier.

Now Lincoln wanted to get off the mountain faster than ever. But his body wasn't cooperating. A climb down a 100-foot (30-meter) rock wall took him two hours. Normally, he could do it in 15 minutes.

Assuming Lincoln was dead, the Sherpas took his water, food, and oxygen and left his body.

This memorial honors the famous mountaineer George Leigh-Mallory. He died in 1924, trying to reach the summit of Mount Everest.

Lincoln was suffering from altitude sickness. His brain was swelling with fluid. The Sherpas gave him bottled oxygen, but it didn't help. Lincoln's body was shutting down. By 7:00 in the evening on May 25, he was unconscious. Lincoln had spent 19 hours in the Death Zone.

The Sherpas tried to wake him up. They even poked him in the eye. Lincoln didn't respond. Assuming Lincoln was dead, the Sherpas took his water, food, and oxygen and left his body.

CRYING IN BED

News of Lincoln's death spread quickly by radio and the Internet. A family friend called Barbara and told her the awful news. Barbara always knew death was a possibility with such a trip. Still, the reality shocked her. She told her sons. They sat together and held hands before going to bed. Nobody in the Hall family slept much that night. They could all hear each other crying in bed.

19

CHAPTER 4

MOUNTAINTOP MIRACLE

LEARN ABOUT:

- Awakening at night
- Discovered on the edge
- Helped back to safety

This is the view Lincoln had from where he was stranded on Mount Everest.

Sometime during the night, Lincoln woke up. He was cold and confused. By some miracle, he remembered where he was. He also remembered his promise to Barbara and the boys. Lincoln did his best to keep warm. He wrapped his arms around his chest, and he moved as much as possible. But he couldn't move too far. Lincoln was trapped on a cliff. If he stumbled off the side, he would fall between 7,000 and 10,000 feet (2,100 and 3,000 meters).

Back in Australia, during one of her rare moments of sleep, Barbara had a dream. She dreamt that Lincoln was still alive.

Meanwhile, a bit lower down on Everest, American climber Dan Mazur was getting his team ready. Mazur was leading two climbers and a Sherpa. They expected to reach the summit by mid-morning. But a surprise awaited them first.

MAN ON A RIDGE

By 7:30 in the morning on May 26, Dan and his climbers had made good progress. The summit was only two hours away. Suddenly, Dan noticed a flash of yellow fabric. As he climbed up the mountain, he realized it was a person. A man was sitting cross-legged on a ridge. He was fumbling with his jacket in an attempt to change into dry clothes. His chest was bare and his fingers were frozen.

The man looked at Dan. "I imagine you're surprised to see me here!" he said.

Yes, Dan was surprised. "Can you tell me your name?" Dan asked.

"Yeah. Yes!" the man said. "I know my name. My name is Lincoln Hall."

Lincoln was cold and confused when he was found.

Dan's team gave Lincoln oxygen from a portable tank like the one seen here.

EDGE FACT

At least 15 people died on Mount Everest in 2006, making it one of the deadliest climbing seasons in history.

HELP NEEDED FAST

Dan radioed Lincoln's climbing team for help. They were shocked that he was alive. Word quickly spread by radio and the Internet that Lincoln had survived the night on Everest. One of his sons saw the news online and showed his mother. Barbara didn't believe it.

Though the news was true, Lincoln wasn't out of danger. He still had altitude sickness, which made it tough to get him off the mountain. Lincoln was weak and confused. He would have to be guided every inch of the way back down the mountain.

Word quickly spread by radio and the Internet that Lincoln had survived the night on Everest.

Lincoln road a yak down the mountain. He was too weak and confused to walk on his own.

Dan's team gave Lincoln oxygen, water, and candy bars. But they knew he needed to get to a lower altitude. Dan and his team decided not to continue on to the summit. Saving Lincoln's life was more important to them. They asked a pair of climbers passing by to help. The climbers claimed to not speak English. Later, Dan learned they did speak English. They simply had wanted to reach the summit.

MOUNTAIN RESCUE

Later that day, 12 Sherpas climbed up to Lincoln's spot. Dan and his team stayed to help. As a group, the rescuers guided Lincoln down 12 miles (19 kilometers) to a lower camp. The trip took 11 hours.

The next day, Lincoln called Barbara. She still couldn't believe her husband was alive. "Is it really you?" she asked. It was.

Lincoln Hall survived the world's most unforgiving mountain. Though luck played a part, Lincoln's physical fitness and life-long training carried him through. He survived freezing temperatures, icy cliffs, and altitude sickness. And through his confusion, a part of Lincoln held on to his promise. He told Barbara and the boys that he would live. In the end, Lincoln Hall kept his word.

Dan Mazur and his climbing team spent four hours caring for Lincoln near the top of Mount Everest.

Lincoln had frostbite damage to his fingers.

GLOSSARY

altitude (AL-tih-tood)—how high a place is above sea level

documentary (dok-yuh-MEN-tuh-ree)—a movie or TV program about real situations and people

expedition (ek-spuh-DISH-uhn)—a journey with a goal, such as reaching the top of a mountain

frostbite (FRAWST-bite)—a condition that occurs when cold temperatures freeze skin

summit (SUHM-it)—the highest point of a mountain

unconscious (uhn-KON-shuhss)—not awake or able to respond to others

visually impaired (VI-zhuh-uh-lee im-PAIRED)—when one's sense of sight is damaged

READ MORE

Kyi, Tanya Lloyd. *Rescues!* True Stories from the Edge. Toronto: Annick Press, 2006.

Markle, Sandra. *Rescues.* Minneapolis: Millbrook Press, 2006.

O'Shei, Tim. *The World's Most Amazing Survival Stories.* The World's Top Tens. Mankato, Minn.: Capstone Press, 2007.

INTERNET SITES

FactHound offers a safe, fun way to find Internet sites related to this book. All of the sites on FactHound have been researched by our staff.

Here's how:

1. Visit *www.facthound.com*

2. Choose your grade level.

3. Type in this book ID **142960090X** for age-appropriate sites. You may also browse subjects by clicking on letters, or by clicking on pictures and words.

4. Click on the **Fetch It** button.

FactHound will fetch the best sites for you!

INDEX